Richard Godfrey

SECRETS, LIES AND LITTLE JOYS

AUSTIN MACAULEY PUBLISHERS™

LONDON • CAMBRIDGE • NEW YORK • SHARJAH

A CIP catalogue record for this title is available from the British Library.

ISBN 9781035832392 (Paperback)
ISBN 9781035832408 (ePub e-book)

www.austinmacauley.com

First Published 2024
Austin Macauley Publishers Ltd®
1 Canada Square
Canary Wharf
London
E14 5AA

Richard Godfrey began his career as a scientist working with elite British sportspeople and is now an academic at a university in southeast England. He was born and brought up in the West of Scotland and began writing poetry in the late 1970s at the age of sixteen, in the hope of understanding the world, himself, finding meaning and of expressing himself in a positive and creative way. This proved to be a very useful outlet, alongside sport, exercise and music, in maintaining physical and mental health and in recovering from the many 'challenges' that are part of life.

To my mother, who died in 1980; I still miss you and hope you are pleasantly surprised and proud of what I have achieved and of what I have become.

True friends are those who wish the best for you and are thrilled when good things happen in your life. Along the way, you learn who these people are; they are few but they really are appreciated and valued. Chief among these in my life are Greg and Penny Whyte. Thank you!

Many thanks to the following for reading the poems, being honest, giving me very useful feedback and constructive criticism, and ultimately, encouraging me to have them published: Rosemary Neilson, Jenni Jones, Linda Alexander, Dan Bishop, Craig Sharp and Isla Whateley.

Many thanks, too, to all at Austin Macauley Publishers for their hard work and advice in getting this book to print.

Table of Contents

Long Haul   18

School Bored!   20

Plymouth Ho!   25

Light   28

La Vie Joyeaux   30

To Be with You   33

Pauvre de Moi   35

Doubt   37

My Last Night in Bordeaux   40

White Cloud   43

The Best Science   45

A Thousand-Year Love   49

Roman Bearsden   51

A Thing of the Past   54

Deceit in Early Spring   56

Training   59

Gum Tree   61

The One   64

Autumn Calls Louder Now   68

Gaius Caligula   71

Pressure   73

Prowess Everlasting   75

Remission's End   77

The Hunted   79

Starbucks vs Costa   81

Suicide?   83

Decisions   85

Land of Hope and Glory   87

Armageddon Earth   89

The Truth of the Matter   91

Winter…Discontent   93

Årlanda   95

Death of a Loved One   97

Masquerade   99

High-Powered Dying   101

New Guitar   103

Frozen Winter Landscape   105

Business Tide   107

North Star   109

Max   111

The 'New' Royal Opera House, Covent Garden   113

Smell   115

Writing	118
Childhood Rain	121
Christmas Flight	123
Addict	125
Doctorate	127
Holocaust Memorial	129
Ignorance Across Millenia	132
Letters	134
Biathlon: The Build-Up Begins	136
Wreck	138
Travel at Night	140
Phoenix	142
Silk	144
GB Biathlon	146
Fully Laden Travel	148
Canada Beckons	150
The Wait	152
Arctic Call	154
Flag	156
At Byron's Grave	158
The Truth Will Out	160
Farewell	162

Why poetry reading and writing is such good self-help

Our lives are rich and varied, and a well-lived life results in secrets, lies and little joys, amongst many other things, along the way. The bottom line is that in navigating life, we are often searching for meaning—the structure of your life and its place in the world in which you live. With that, we often look for an explanation for the way life unfolds, why we react the way we do and the way others—parents, siblings, friends, teachers and bosses, for example—react the way they do. The sad thing is that we can often feel isolated by the sense we are alone in our dealings with the world and our place in it. The truth is in, almost, every case, this is not true.

Hundreds of thousands of people have had similar experiences but very few choose to reflect in writing, relating these experiences and the feelings they invoke, to an audience. The poems presented here and the explanations, comments and commentaries that go alongside them were recently described by someone I have known for 45 years as being 'powerful, raw and incredibly honest'.

In many cases, I have reflected on, confronted and dealt with difficulties in my own life in such a way that I have been able to move on with less baggage weighing me down. In dealing with things, being an imperfect human being, as we all are, I have rarely dealt with things perfectly.

One major means of understanding the world, being more appreciative of beauty in life and for coping in a world that is predominantly hard and unfair has been, for me, to write poetry. I have written many poems over the years. I began as a sixteen-year-old and still write now in my sixties.

I had a few difficulties in my teenage years, and when I was eighteen, my mother died, but even before that the usual teenage anxieties—schoolwork, girls, conflict with parents, teachers and other authority figures and my mother's longstanding ill health—all contributed to me starting to self-harm when I was 15. I would cut myself with a knife, or use the tip of a knife to rub away skin until it bled. I am not proud of that but I don't condemn it. There are many people who self-harm, unable to cope, they discover this distraction from other real and imagined pain and, once it becomes a habit, it can 'inhabit' you too. The pain and drawing of blood can cause a release of emotions that can become addictive. But it's really not the way forward!

I am pleased to say that I never reached that addictive stage. I was lucky to discover poetry writing instead and if there is anyone at the early stages of self-harm, I would urge you to write down your feelings instead. It is a much better way and has additional benefits, such as increasing your sense of empowerment and of pride that can come with knowing you are being creative, not destructive. Some readers may be interested to know that nowadays, it is not uncommon for psychiatrists to prescribe courses of creative writing because in the 1980s, it was discovered to be efficacious treatment for many with depression. But, of course, we now know it is good, not just treatment, but also for prevention of many mental health issues.

At sixteen, first I attempted to write prose to encapsulate the fear, pain and emotion that I felt. Also, anguish! This sounds so melodramatic, when I write it, but that word is defined by Google Dictionary as 'severe mental or physical pain and suffering' and this is, genuinely, what I felt as a teenager. Prose, however, seemed far too slow a way for me to express myself and so I discovered poetry writing, really as a short-hand, quicker means to get out emotion, which felt like it might destroy me. So, I could put it on paper instead and so, importantly, both physically and metaphorically, I could put these feelings to one side. This became a ritual which was very useful and meant I was far less likely to dwell on difficulties in my life, not allowing me to harbour feelings which could so easily have festered, and could have grown out of control.

In prosody (versification / poetry), I was surprised to become aware that I had clearly paid attention in Mrs Bell's third-year English classes at school on poetry, and learnt something that I was now 'accidently' applying—rhyme, meter, alliteration, cesura, enjambment, and so on. Reference to other works, notably the Bible, Shakespeare, but other poets too, the Romantics, Bacon, Donne, Nabokov, Whitman, Burns *ad libitum* and *ad nauseum*. Suddenly, this too gave me an interest in and greater enjoyment of literature more widely.

But honestly, I wish I had read much more widely from that point onwards, on history and in literature. I didn't, and it is only now that I voluntarily engage in reading those things suggested in watching psychologists, scientists, philosophers and writers on YouTube and so I am now starting to read

Jung, Solzhenitsyn, Dickens and am contemplating Dostoevsky! The truth is my pile of books waiting to be read is growing too fast and I am reading too slowly.

I could go on, but the point is that I want to recognise, and wish I'd had the chance to thank, Mrs Bell, the brilliant English teacher I had when I was 14 years of age. She never knew it, but I feel it no exaggeration to say she first gave me the means to save my own life. But more than that, she opened up a vast exciting, interesting world which, to my shame, I have not explored widely enough. But I also discovered I could be creative and that I could think laterally more than most. This has helped me as a professional scientist, teacher, 'thinker' and sometimes discoverer of new things. It empowered me and gave me a sense of pride. So, Mrs Bell, sincerely, thank you!

To a large degree, all of my poetry writing was for *me* and served a preeminent and pragmatic purpose, that of catharsis. I have of course, written a few for others, a girlfriend here and there, to impress, influence and often to express genuine love and affection and so, since generally, I was writing for myself, truly contemplating publication, sharing my thoughts in writing, is something I have only occasionally thought about, and so, attempting to publish poetry has come quite late in my life.

So, to reiterate, my poems are inspired by many things but when all is stripped away, the vast majority are about making sense of the world and my place in it. In this first collection, I have included poems on growing up, on wildlife, weather, work, relationships, love, loss of love and unrequited love. And have used writing when I needed it most for those times when you need all your strength to recover from hurt, avoid the storm, dodge the 'void', as I think of death, to generally steer away from catastrophe.

Your upbringing by your parents, your personality, the experiences you have, their consequences and how you deal with them, all shape who you are. However, although we are perhaps sculpted in childhood and young adulthood, if we have open minds, and aspire to honour, honesty and integrity, we are as we should be; life-long learners with compassion for and empathy with others and the world around us. None of us is perfect, and I epitomise human imperfection but I still try to make time to view the world with awe, to think, to improve, to try to be a better person and to be grateful.

In a Sunday Times article many years ago, I read with interest a 'review' of the personality of poets, suggesting they write what they feel and see, often with little regard for the sensitivities of others. And so condemned; the truth is that both good and cruel thoughts are capable of expression through poetry and, they are in mine too. I am not always proud of the thoughts I have expressed in my poetry. As Jung observed on the human psyche, generally:

'…every one possesses something of the criminal, the genius, and the saint within…'

Writing poetry allows you to explore these areas of your character, to attempt to make sense of life, without judgement, without the risks that immediately writing it on social media or the Internet can bring.

Long Haul

Endless flight, or so it seems;
Twelve hours to Kuala Lumpur.
Then short respite,
Sydney beckons but I struggle and I fight!

Jump the Java Sea,
Jakarta to the west,
Answerable to no-one,
Except the wind's behest.

Antipodes ahead, Australia looming large,
An isle the size of Europe, soon to take charge.
I think of Cairns, the Great Barrier Reef,
Seen from the stars, staggering belief.

In my previous job, I worked as a scientist in support of elite athletes. As a result, I did a lot of travelling, including a number of trips to Australia, which is a fantastic place. Getting there from the UK however, can be torture. It's quite uncomfortable to be stuck in a seat with poor leg room and so, with inadequate chances for much movement, long flights are seemingly never ending.

On this trip, the flight was broken with a short stopover in Kuala Lumpur, Malaysia. On the back of each seat of the plane is a small video screen so you can chart the progress of the flight, superimposed on the map of the region. So, it's not that my knowledge of geography is great, because I cheated! But the flight's progress on the map was the spark for this poem.

School Bored!

I sit in sombre, sober, silence
The drone of her voice
A dirge of white noise
I hope to ride to the most isolated
Inner reaches of my mind.
And once there explore
A bright and interesting world
Far from this land of boring grey Victorian drab.
I am reminded of the greyest winter dawn of my childhood
Glasgow.

But deep inside my own mind
I explore the richest of lands and of weather;
The rolling hills of Darwin, Eldredge and Gould
Of gentle reiteration of evolution's tenets.
The foothills of Nabokov
And the fascination that is comparative zoology and
taxonomy.
The abrasive winds of Dawkins;
Darwin's Rottweiler, staunch and resolute,
If a little deluded,
Defender of phyletic gradualism.
The bright sunshine of treasure that is the Natural History
Museum
And that bright blue sky of boundless horizon
The Darwin Centre.

I think of the Jurassic Coast in Dorset

And imagine, geology hammer in hand,

Strolling along the beach between Lyme and Charmouth,

Listening for the ghost of Mary Anning, while

Perfect ammonites and belemnites vie for attention amongst the pebbles,

And graptolite-patterned rock reminds me we once studied Didymograptus.

It is a cool, bright, sunny day and a breeze full of salt and seaweed

Carries my mind to rockpools of anemones and sea urchins,

Starfish and blennies, crabs and mussels, barnacles and clams.

Bladderwrack, drying-out in the sun and air feels slimy to the touch.

And it is good to be alive enjoying nature's bounty, if only in my head,

So far from the useless gas-bagging of self-important meetingophiles.

How rich the landscape of the mind and the escape it provides.

The university where I work used to be organised in 'schools' and every few months I had to attend a meeting of our school board whose only function was to ratify the decisions of other committees. As a consequence, it was not an exciting event and on one occasion, seeking escape, I wrote this poem.

The second verse perhaps needs some explanation. Darwin, of course, was the founder (co-founder, actually; with Alfred Russell Wallace) of the theory of Evolution by Natural Selection. Eldredge and Gould modified Darwin's original theory with the publication of their own treatise on 'Punctuated Equilibrium' in 1972, 113 years after 'On the Origin of Species' was published. Eldredge and Gould's contention was accepted that, in evolution, everything continues not just with gradual change over time; so-called 'phyletic gradualism' of Natural Selection, but is occasionally also punctuated by a rapid, or revolutionary change.

Nabokov is the Russian author who wrote 'Lolita', amongst other prose and poetry. He was an entomologist and, in the 1940s, curator of lepidoptery (study of butterflies and moths) at Harvard University's Museum of Comparative Zoology. He was the discoverer of a few new species of butterfly and moth and had a whole genus named after him— the *Nabokovia*. One of his poems, 'On Discovering a Butterfly', describes his pleasure in being a lepidopterist and placing a red label on a butterfly specimen to denote it the 'holotype', the defining, first-discovered of a species.

I describe the prolific writer of popular science books and evolutionary biologist, Richard Dawkins, from the University of Oxford who occupied the position of Simonyi Professor for the Public Understanding of Science as 'Darwin's rottweiler'. Dawkins is a quite ferocious atheist and defender, and explainer, of Natural Selection and its links to random mutation. My description of Dawkins here is a 'nod' to Thomas Huxley the Victorian naturalist and contemporary of Darwin's. In the year following the 1859 publication of 'On the Origin of Species' Darwin was roundly ridiculed. Huxley was a great defender of the theory, and of Darwin, and, accordingly, the press of the time named him 'Darwin's bulldog'.

On 30th June 1860 in the University of Oxford's own Natural History Museum, Huxley debated Samuel Wilberforce on the theory of Natural Selection. Samuel Wilberforce was the grandson of the British slave abolitionist, William Wilberforce, and whom the press had nicknamed 'Soapy Sam'. It is said, the debate was so heated that women in the room fainted! In 2000, I was lucky enough to deliver a lecture in that same room on my work with elite athletes, invited by the university, to help mark its celebration of Science, Engineering and Technology week.

In the third verse, I mention Mary Anning (1799-1847). She was born into a poor family in Lyme Regis and they sold the fossils they found in the nearby coastal cliffs, of what we often now refer to as the 'Jurassic Coast'. As she grew up, Anning became famous as an expert on fossils and many eminent scientists of the day sought her advice but few ever gave her credit. The Natural History Museum in South Kensington in London today has a permanent tribute to her along with many of the ichthyosaur fossils she discovered. She unfortunately died of breast cancer at the age of 48 in 1847. This too struck a chord with me as my mother died at age 49 of another cancer that only females can suffer from, ovarian cancer.

An additional, interesting note: Darwin and Anning never met as far as we know and despite great overlap in their work, Darwin, Anning and Mendel (famous for discoveries on genetics) were, I think, unaware of each other's work. But they all lived at the same time, or at least overlapped—Darwin (1809-1882), Anning (1799-1847) and Mendel (1822-1884).

Plymouth Ho!

We stepped into the November sea
And, for twenty-five metres, waded, thick
Leathery, slippery kelp licking round our thighs, knees,
ankles, calves
Waves growing with every step further

Into a murky brown and frothy rising tide.
Wind blew, blowing, spewing waves and spray
Towards weather-beaten, hard grey jagged rocks.
But not cold in black and blue neoprene.

Yet still, the heart beats fast
Breath comes in a short, sharp gasp
Excitement heightened with each and every growing wave
No music creates greater rhythm, greater rave.

A good friend of mine G has worked as the physical challenge advisor to all the celebrities who have completed challenges to raise money for Comic Relief and Sport Relief. When one of them was training to swim the channel, one Saturday morning we caught a series of trains, starting very early in the morning. In Plymouth we went sea swimming. G had told his wife not worry as there would be a safety boat. When we got there, it was too rough for a safety boat. We struggled into our wetsuits and swam anyway! There was a camera filming and so I was asked not to swim with G and his 'trainee' and so I swam out, in a slightly different direction, out of sight of the camera. It wasn't long before I began feeling that swimming on my own was probably not a good idea!

So, I swam back and, thinking it might be easier to get out at a rocky promontory, I headed for it. The waves carried me in and I grabbed the rocks but as the waves receded, I was plucked off. It took three attempts and, on the third occasion, it was only by gripping hard with my hands, knees and feet, and with lucky timing before the receding water pulled me back with it, I just managed to scramble out. It is really exciting to swim in conditions like that but you need to be very fit (fitter than I am now!) have good safety precautions in place and even then, be aware; open water swimming, particularly sea-swimming in late autumn in UK coastal waters, is not without its risks!

Light

With a jolt I am
Alive once more in your company
Again, in the light

I read an interesting book on the Japanese poetry discipline of Haiku and now have had quite a few attempts. Not easy, as traditionally the poem is supposed to be just three lines of 17 syllables; five in the first and third line and seven in the second line. Modernisation of this style still insists on three lines expressed with 'pithy' concision but the number of syllables need not be so strict. The exercise for me was to attempt to convey something as succinctly and economically as possible and Haiku is the very epitome of economy.

La Vie Joyeaux

Life excites: the rush of a first experience
Excites every fibre, every cell,
When embracing that new sensation, anticipating the next
tingling thrill,
A rich and rolling landscape in which to summit every hill.

Smell excites: fresh ground coffee; evocation of past
memories,
The joy of discovering the beauty of tree blossom scent;
Lime divine, hanging on the breeze,
Forsaking breathing for hedonistic olfactory wheeze.

Sound excites: stirring nature in the early morn,
At first; quiet murmurings in the dark. But at first light,
Crescendo chorus greets the spring and summer dawn.
Rising from quiet slumber humans blink and stretch and
yawn.

Sound excites: on first hearing Santana's 'Smooth';
The tingle down my spine, the prickling of my skin,
The watering of my mouth; sharp, satisfying stab
As I revel; seeking to prolong pleasure therein.
Sight excites: the frustratingly beautiful Banded Demoiselle;
Flitting by the river's edge, in wend and weave and tack,
Evading the hunting camera lens
Taunting metallic blue, and shiny black-eyed awareness
staring back.

Sight excites: to see a sunrise over a vista
Not seen before. To feel breathless at the sight.
Of a topaz moon; slowly, deliberately, unhesitantly, rising
From behind a tree-studded hill where shadows seem to fight.

Sight excites: in quiet 'dark sky sites' when spying the Milky
Way;
To thrill to each and every bright and twinkling star
With heartbeat moments and awe-filled thought of distance,
time and space
Confronted with that panorama; the insignificance of the
Human Race.

Modern life is very busy and everyone is encouraged to cram more and more into the working day. I needed to remind myself, in the interest of a better work-life balance, that away from work, there is much to be grateful for and to take pleasure in. Recognising and acknowledging these things can really help and can combat stress.

To Be with You

Your eyes of stunning Mediterranean blue
I bathe there in the deep.
Your fine hair of gold like powder sand
Where lies the shipwreck of my heart
And its secrets do you keep.

Close beside; my soul washed up
Half dead, upon your golden shore
But soon I seek reality
And can hold my tongue no more.

I seek no mere existence
I search for the open door
And into an island realm of light
In warmth, I would hold you once more.

I've always been interested in, but generally unlucky with, women. I'm getting older now and so, looking back, I guess I've been lucky enough to have had a few relationships. Some good, some bad but often great fun, very loving and very educational. I am not sure I am great at giving and receiving love and it's only as I have grown older and more experienced, I have begun to understand what is important, how not to be too self-conscious and how to be more considerate of and to others. I'm still working on it!

There are times I felt unworthy and may have 'scuppered' things unknowingly and even on occasion knowingly. But I am not sure I learnt enough, at least not as much as I could and should have and not quickly enough to avoid 'missing my window'! Perhaps there are many lessons here, not least of which on knowing a good thing when you've got it?

Pauvre de Moi

You tell anyone who will listen
That you still love me.
But since we split
Post-traumatic stress has knocked on my door.

An irrational fear grips me at the thought
Of you ringing my doorbell
Late at night, or the prospect of our meeting in the street.
Your wretched behaviour drove me to this point.

And you talk of love. In reality you miss
The company of a man who treated you with love and respect
And admired you for your achievements.
You miss what has passed and you miss an imagined future.

But that is not love, however strongly felt.
Love is full of willing compromise,
Unselfish acts, of mutual trust and of respect.
But all you see and feel emanates from you; La Pauvre.

Sometimes we meet someone who is wrong for us. In this case the subject of this poem was probably wrong for most people! Beware those who refer to themselves as a 'victim', that the world is against them, that bad things always single them out and the person who is unable to admit they might occasionally be wrong, or who never says 'sorry'. Every life has its ups and downs and it is important to enjoy and be grateful for the good times and respect and appreciate the bad times. It is those people who despite every 'challenge' still describe themselves as 'survivors' and who see good in everyone and everything, with a bit of healthy scepticism, not too much naivety, don't take themselves too seriously and have a sense of humour that are the most fun to be around. This poem could have had the alternative title of 'Stalker', but that is a whole other story.

Doubt

<u>August</u>; feeling quite unwell
I tell my friends 'This feels like
more than just a hangover!'
You wanker! You've just drunk too much!'

Their dismissal and derision, although hardly unreasonable, hurts.
I shut my mouth, the nausea remains and the worry grows
Along with increasing bouts
Of burning 'indigestion'.

<u>September</u>; six weeks later
I have a heart attack and a cardiac arrest
And, thanks to paramedics, I am hauled back from the brink
But even then, those doubters remain doubters.

<u>May</u>; nineteen months later; breathlessness and dizziness reign.
My best friend, chief among doubters, tells me I'm just unfit,
I should get my finger out and get to the gym more often.
But even eating is hard because of the breathlessness, so the gym?
<u>July</u>; seven weeks later
I collapse at home and, when I regain consciousness,
It is to extreme breathlessness and light headedness.
In hospital, blood clots are found in both my lungs,

A prelude to another fight for life.
But what is it about me that
Causes doubters to doubt, to question my credibility?
And now a new fear arises.

I fear that despite severe symptoms
That testify to an imminent challenge to my life
In the future, again, I will not be believed
And this time I will die.

Why?… Am I simply dismissed as a 'drama queen'?
Or someone who exaggerates, or is an attention seeker?
Perhaps, to the doubters, my death and funeral
Will prove I <u>was</u> an attention seeker!
Life is truly more perverse than I perceive.

Amongst males growing up, particularly if they do a lot of team sport, in that subculture we grow up with a lot of 'banter'. Dismissal, 'ribbing', teasing, ridicule and other behaviours are not unusual but are rarely vindictive. In this poem, basically you can see I wasn't taken seriously—nobody's fault, but unfortunately, a few weeks later, I ended up having a heart attack!

My Last Night in Bordeaux

I noticed her upon entering the dining room,
The pretty waitress who took my order.
Given in French, which she accepted
As if delivered by a French aristocrat.

Yet we both knew it was deeply flawed
And this served only to sharpen the twinkle in my eye.
A polite and unassuming woman, with many hues,
Many currents beneath a calm surface, I feel sure.

For how else to deal with Brits who refuse even
To attempt the bad French I dare utter?
She turns to deliver my order to the kitchen
And confirms she is of callipygian aspect.

But that too I'd noticed from the first casual glance
And there and then the truth untold; déjà vu:
I thought, 'I need a woman like you,
To teach me the nature of romance, of a love that's true.'

For many years I've searched and had many false hopes
extinguished
Although, at times, hope is rekindled by such beauty,
I suspect a fallow field is all that stands between now and my
demise
But in my heart a spark remains despite the heavy glance of
others that seem simply to despise

A view which hangs and they seem unwilling to disguise
And yet nowadays I struggle less with my conscience
As I do not feel admiration of the female form
Should necessarily mean consignment to second class
citizenry.

A wandering eye? Harmless, I never acted inappropriately but for some reason, foreign women have always had appeal, and it's not just me and it's not new, and as proof—the Ancient Roman poet Ovid (full name: Publius Ovidius Naso, who lived from 43 BC-18 AD) noted when reporting on a festival that drew people from far and wide:

'All of Rome was in a whirl
Enraptured by some foreign girl'

White Cloud

White cloud was forecast for today
And yet, for the last four hours, a warm and low-slung sun
Has hung from a bright blue sky, devoid of cloud,
But welcomed by a smiling population
Desperate to escape the oppression of dreary winter.

But with a chill befitting January, I check the forecast.
On the BBC website
The words 'white cloud',
With an appropriately descriptive image,
Stare resolutely back.

I stand to look out of the window
And peer far and wide
To spot the white cloud that must soon
Surely envelope us, plunging the world once more,
Into a depressingly dreary murk.

But strain as I might,
My neck and my eyes,
I simply cannot locate said 'white cloud'
And I am heartened.
An almost piece of summer lightening the mood.

As a Brit, I always have one eye on the weather. Having been born and brought up in the West of Scotland, dry days are a novelty and often in spring, my favourite season, I have been known to drop everything to go walking in the sunshine in the big outdoors. Sure, this means I'll have to catch-up on work later, when the weather is less appealing or it's dark! Perhaps that is a better way to live—in the moment. We spend far too long 'angsting' over the past or worrying about the future and both can be the source of great stress and anxiety. Planning can undoubtedly be very useful and allows us to fit more into an increasingly busy life. It has taken me a long time to learn, but I am getting better at being more spontaneous and living in the moment and I plan to do so more and more.

The Best Science

The best science,
The most rewarding science,
The science that excites the researcher,
The science that creates thirst for knowledge

Is that where the outcome is completely unknown;
There is no room for speculation,
For estimating the magnitude of the expected response.
And in that realm

There is no previous data to allow estimation
Of the number of participants required
To achieve appropriate statistical power.
It is precisely that unknown which MAKES science 'rock'.

The thrill of examining the findings
Only glimpsed, in any form when
The data have been analysed and interrogated
And slowly, slowly is revealed the outcome.

For some time, I have been worrying about the future of science. Since its inception in the 1660s (no, I wasn't around then!), although not perfect the scientific method has resulted in the inexorable progress of human beings. From the discovery of antibiotics which saw the extension of lifespan, to computing, to the clothes we stand up in and construction and decoration of houses, to the development of electric cars, a steering away from fossil fuels which, if we are lucky may save the planet.

So, anyone who says 'we have had enough of experts', is a fool. Scientists, that 1.4% of the UK population with a PhD (a research degree), are experts and there would be no technology and no progress without science. We should embrace science and experts and fund it wholeheartedly. The problem is that the non-experts do not even know the right questions to ask to solve important problems and so without experts, humans and all life on our planet will perish....it might still do so anyway!

Most people who are not trained in science do not understand it. They, and I include most of the members of the general public, most journalists, most MPs, and many of those with an undergraduate degree in science, really don't get it. This is deeply worrying as this ignorance has a profound effect on society and unfortunately it is e-media influencers, and decision makers, without training in identifying good (objective and verifiable) evidence from subjective opinion and feelings. Most of these people think, if it is written in a science textbook, then it is written in stone, immutable.

Scientific theories rely on the current weight of evidence. Where evidence is considered 'weighty' enough, it contributes to a theory that can become accepted by science. If one new piece of research evidence suggests that the current accepted theory may be incorrect, then the theory can be modified, and or thrown out, in favour of a new theory. In this way science is self-correcting and progress occurs over time.

In the desire to have everything driven by the acquisition of money, we are losing sight of what is important. And so, peer-reviewed journals are now loathed to accept data which is the result of a study that is 'simply' a repeat of one that has been done before because new data, that has arisen from original research, is perceived to sell better. This must not be allowed to continue further.

Traditionally, scientists have been taught that writing a good, detailed methodology section is important because it allows other researchers to independently repeat the study and by so doing, refute or confirm the originally collected data. This refutation or confirmation is one of the cornerstones of the scientific method and is the basis of science itself.

With respect to the contents of this poem; the statistical power of a study relates to its p value. Often research studies are carried out on a smaller subset of the population that may be characterised by the outcome of the research. To do this the participants must collectively be a random representation of the larger population you wish to gain information on or knowledge of. The study is carried out on that representative subset and data are statistical analysed. Resulting p values are found and only the cut-offs of 0.05 and 0.09 (i.e. p≤0.05 or p≤0.09) are accepted by science as statistically significant. In other words, the probability of the findings being true for the larger population is 95% (p= 0.05) and 99% (p= 0.09). This is a very high standard.

Often in science a 'power calculation' can be performed where, using previous research data, the magnitude of an expected outcome can be estimated and used in a calculation to identify the number of participants required to achieve a p value at a certain level. This is a perfectly valid thing to do but it does in my opinion increase the risks of experimenter bias. So, having no idea what the likely outcome might be, produces findings that are much less likely to be biased. It also retains more 'mystery' and provides greater excitement where any speculation on the outcome can be more independent.

A Thousand-Year Love

I'll love you for a thousand years
The rhythm of your soul
A constant echo in my heart
Fills a life of deprivation, a life that longs to start.

For without you I am empty
Only you can fill this void
For now, this existence is without virtue
And with love I've only toyed.

You complete the cycle
In which I am renewed
I'll give you all my life and love
And forever more with happiness be imbued.

When I am in, I'm all in! I have tendency to perhaps overinvest and like too many of us, have often equated happiness with not being alone. This too is fading as I age and can enjoy my own company more readily and easily. Of course, the more time you spend alone the less able you are to compromise and modify the bad habits you've developed, and so now, of course, I have less choice. Who would have me?

Roman Bearsden

Many sites in Bearsden now call me
To examine a Roman past that seems
So intertwined with my own past.
A history of 40 years enmeshed with one of 1900 years.

For me it began in ignorance when, as children,
We played football using the stones marking the line
Of the Antonine Wall, as goal posts.
Ignorant of and with no feel for the past or its history.

We'd even squeeze through the railings encircling the exposed
Foundation and vallum to retrieve our ball
But with no real understanding of what lay beneath our feet.
But now I do and am saddened that preservation has been neglected

In that place since my childhood.
Roman history was revealed again in 1973 when at Bearsden Cross,
Under the foundations of demolished Victorian Houses,
A Roman fort was unearthed.
My imagination was stimulated as the scorch marks from an open fire
Was pointed out on the floor of what was once a barracks.
In my mind's eye I saw the soldiers at their gaming boards
And heard their noisy cheering as bets were won and lost.

But at age 12 the image was not as crisp and sharp as it is now.
True I have since read much of the Roman occupation
Of our islands, but why the history now lives, I am at a loss to explain.
But I am keen to explore the numerous sites in this one small town.

I grew up in a town just north-west of Glasgow called Bearsden. In AD142, Emperor Antonine had a wall built on the then frontier, coast to coast between the Firth of Forth, (east of Edinburgh), and the Firth of Clyde, (west of Glasgow). Bearsden was a military fort on the wall. On Roman Road, in the town, was a line of old, derelict Victorian detached houses. In 1973 they were demolished and, a few feet under the foundations of these Victorian houses, was found a Roman barracks and bathhouse.

Archaeologists from the University of Glasgow led a dig there and many artefacts were found—they are now housed in the university's Hunterian Museum. As a 12-year-old schoolboy, I was taken on a school trip to see the dig. The bathhouse is to this day preserved as a monument but all the other parts were filled-in and a three-storey block of flats built on the site. When I return to visit family, I very often go there and sit on a bench by the bathhouse and soak up the atmosphere.

A Thing of the Past

Am I resurrected?
Is my troubled pain all gone?
I search the archives of my mind,
Two decades past, so almost to another life belong.

Is the bonfire spent?
The embers sometimes flare,
But not conflict from the past's revisit,
No evil eyes that stare.

What's past is past
That time is now long gone
No echoes do I hear
And now with content, springing stride, I pace
From year to year.

My teenage years were quite turbulent, but then that is true for many people. In my early teens, my mother was often ill, secondary school was not always great for a mixed-race child in the 1970s and I had the usual teenage angst and awkwardness that made finding female company difficult / impossible. I began self-harm but fortunately discovered poetry writing as a better; more creative and less destructive, means of channelling frustration.

Twenty years later, when in my mid-thirties, I still had a few issues but they were far less frequent. It seems I had managed those issues reasonably well. I guess the fact I was still alive was a good sign of the benefits of creative writing, of sport and exercise and of karate—all of which I embraced in my early teens.

Deceit in Early Spring

I smelt it first;
The damp on the freshening
Westerly breeze.
The sun now shielded by cloud

Shed golden shafts of light, escaping the cloud at its edges,
Which glistened and sparkled on the river, dancing like rain
drops,
Evoking thoughts and images of rain
Long before any rain actually fell.

In early Spring, Nature loves to taunt
The hopeful and the foolish.
To catch out those wearing
Only a t-shirt, or those failing to carry an umbrella.

When the rain finally came it was ephemeral.
Lasting barely five minutes. Well-spaced drops
Creating concentric circles of river ripples,
Blurring the reflections of trees

And enhancing daydreams, as thoughts and memories
Came and went with the flow of the river,
With the chaos of water which can't stay still
In its urgency to embrace new life; almost imperceptible but
unstoppable.

As with the river the tide of life will ebb and flow
But Spring is hurley, burley, breathless excitement
And very soon life begins to digress; soon ebb will go
And life will grow and grow, leaving only flow.

I love spring and nature, and natural history generally, and enjoy being 'geeky', knowing a few Latin names for some plants, many animals and particularly arthropods (insects and spiders). But knowing Latin names is a bit of a party trick and frankly it is a bit vacuous if that knowledge is isolated.

Connected knowledge is always so much more interesting and brings any interest alive. As the particle physicist Richard Feynman once said, 'Any subject becomes interesting if you scrape below the surface.' So, what do the Latin names refer to i.e. why are they so named? What other facts are there about the species, such as its diet, its behaviour, its physiology, its reproduction, its environment, what other creatures, plants and landscape do they interact with?

I could spend a whole day outside, looking for or at wildlife, observing and taking photos. A tip: in late spring or in summer, spend 10 minutes simply staring at a bush. At first you will see nothing and then things creep into your peripheral vision and you begin to wonder how you missed such obvious, plentiful life.

Training

Each day with exercise is met;
The toil, the grind, the pain, the sweat.
In sunshine, fog, snow and mist and even when it's raining.
What makes the day a better day? When it includes good training.

The gym calls me on many a day,
I kneel and sing and burn and pray
The pain is now friend retiring
But that tolerance, that adaptation, only comes, with repeated training.

When I am sad or grumpy,
Angry, hurt or punchy
I seek to be robbed of breath for complaining,
It's easy, I find distraction in my training.

My body grows in strength,
My thews swell like gourds
Perhaps I can see the sanity I'm retaining,
No drugs, just hard work; a life in deference to good training.

Sport and exercise have always been a refuge, cathartic fire, protector, manager of frustration, and aggression and stimulator of my imagination, focus of aspiration and of awe, especially when I was growing up. But also, birthplace of friendships and career. If you have a problem, go and exercise. When you have finished, the problem will not be gone but it may feel more manageable.

The other benefit of being 'fit' is that you can do more in life with less stress and, in that way, be better able to live in the moment. That is where happiness lives, not dwelling on past mistakes nor worrying about what the future might hold.

Gum Tree

Hot bright blue sunshine
Gave way to heavy rain
And dark grey clouds.
Palm fronds running and dripping water
From green shiny fingers.

The following morning as the heat grew
Mist gave way to steam
The smell of damp wood hanging heavy
And the rich, sweet, peppery smell of the gum tree

Intoxicating, lingering, completely appealing
Draws my imagination
To float on a 1000-year cloud
Back to ancient times.

I found the natural history, climate and landscape of Australia awe-inspiring, but add to that the evocative smell of Aussie jungle after rain; sun-warming-after-damp-peppery-wood. Cities in Australia feel like they are microscopic fringes at the edge of pristine, primaeval wilderness, the very landscape seems to pulse and beat. Where Aussies grow up, being aware of the danger of the indigenous wildlife, tourists are not. When we were preparing athletes for the Summer Olympics in Sydney in 2000, we spent seven weeks for three years in a row on the Gold Coast, near Brisbane, having athletes train and gain experience of the environment.

In that preparation, I used the fact that I had studied two years of zoology at Uni and gave a talk to coaches and medical staff about the dangerous fauna that we all need to be aware of and how to live safely alongside them. There are more dangerous birds, mammals, spiders, insects and snakes than anywhere else in the world, and many staff and athletes were planning holiday after training and after Olympics.

As an example, in the northern suburbs of Sydney, the Sydney funnel web spider (*Atrax robustus*) lives in people's gardens. This spider is aggressive and is reputed to have the most potent venom of any other spider in the world. If bitten, envenomation with δ-atracotoxin and TTX (tetrodotoxin) by this species requires that you seek medical attention and use antivenin within 20 minutes. Sutherland in 1978 characterised a two-phase syndrome that results from envenomation. In summary, the first phase causes extreme pain, difficulties with breathing and over-secretion of bodily fluids, the second phase begins with the victim beginning to feel better but then they die.

All along the north coast of Australia between October to May are swarms of box jellyfish (*Chironex fleckeri*) which actively hunt small fish and ensnare them with up to 7m long tentacles that are covered in nematocysts, stinging cells that deliver sufficient venom to kill 3 grown men. Simply wearing ladies' tights will provide sufficient protection against stinging. We warned athletes so they could take precautions when they went on holiday.

Towards the end of one trip, when we were 'dismantling' the camp, we had more spare time for leisure and on one or two evenings, we would have a jacuzzi in the evening and while drinking a glass of local white wine, we would wander outside in white towelling bathrobes to watch huge flocks of fruit bats flying towards the trees on the periphery of the resort, to roost.

The One

For six months I've lived without you,
Six months we've been apart,
Each day I've lived with thoughts of you,
In the silence of my room, to the beating of my heart.

I cannot shake the feeling
That our destinies are one.
However hard I try to reject the thought
I believed you were, The One.

Through fog and mist
And twists of pain
All attempts to forget you
Are in tatters left, in vain.

I like this poem; I think it has a reasonable rhyming scheme and a pleasing rhythm and it captures the emotion felt at the time. And, at that time it did feel like I loved the woman who this poem is about. But even now it leaves a bad taste in my mouth. There are however, lessons to be learnt from this and it was a hard lesson that made me profoundly sad and unhappy for quite a while. This is seen in the fact that this was written six months after the fact, and yet the depth of emotion was still significant, still 'raw'!

It is a sad fact that most relationships are transient. That is, they do not last. In my case I have never been married, so I have had a number of girlfriends over a number of decades. At the time most felt special and that the relationship might last. Quite a few lasted two or three years, but most didn't. And in most cases the hurt, the pain of loss, did not last six months.

In any relationship, there is give and take and hopefully, the depth of emotion one individual feels for the other is closely matched in the way they feel about you. Where there is mismatch in this strength of feeling, there is increased risk that it might not last and indeed, that is often why a relationship ends. If you have children and or you are married, there is generally a far greater willingness, and need, to try to work things out.

The poem this relationship refers to, is one in which both parties were very keen and this was constantly reinforced by romantic overtures on both sides; by making the other person feel wanted, respected, valued and special. The woman who was the object of my affection here simply stopped responding to any of my communications, and so the term 'ghosted' applies. To this day, 12 years later, I do not know why she ended our relationship. But, in fact, that is the point, she never did 'end it', she just stopped seeing me and ended all contact.

At the end of any relationship, pain, to a greater or lesser degree, is inevitable but the phrase 'letting someone down gently' is important. It captures the fact that if you are the one ending the relationship, it will be very much harder for the other party and so, you need to be humane and try not to hurt the other person more than you need to. Despite the difficulty of doing this face to face, that is what needs to happen, you need to try to give reasons which are not too crushing and phrase things in a way that is not too brutal. But part of this also requires honesty and it being clearly stated that, if you are the person ending the relationship, you wish things to end and not to go any further. These things must be clear and although, it seems brutal, it is perhaps being 'cruel to be kind'.

With 'ghosting' the person being 'dumped', does not even know that is what is happening and so they never have 'closure'. They cling to the hope that the relationship has not ended and they live with that false hope for far too long because the person who should do so has not taken the trouble to be explicit about the ending of the relationship. So, it is not the fault of the person being 'dumped' here and they really are a victim.

'Ghosting' marks the perpetrator out as being cruel, selfish, lacking backbone and moral fibre. So, if we are prepared to, and lucky enough to, enjoy a relationship, we must behave like an adult. Be caring and apply empathy and integrity; end it face to face, preferably in person and, as the person ending the relationship have the guts to 'face the music'! As my mother used to say "Do unto others as you would have done unto you". In other words, treat others as you would like to be treated.

Autumn Calls Louder Now

After crossing the bridge over the river,
The cold air seems to make the very plants quiver.
Damp road, gutter littered with shiny horse chestnut conkers.
My mind wanders, in post viral fog, some thoughts clearly
'bonkers'.

I keep my hands in pockets, seeking to keep them warm
But a thin, damp, cold cagoul is not adequate, but keeps them
from harm
As I stand admiring the scene. The maize field stood tall with
stalks
Just a week ago. But now when the wind blows, the field no
longer rustles and talks.

Now stubbly straw stands, devastated, in symmetrical lines
Even rooks seem perturbed picking at the ground, with
whistles, caws and whines.
In the far distance, snail slow, cars crawl
With a backdrop of green wooded hills, they transport and
haul.

In woodland, still some summer green
Where muntjac and roe deer roam, where badger and fox stop
to preen.
The landscape damp, the gentle rain continues falling
Autumn is the barrier that has Winter stalling

Between the fields a wire-strung fence; between this and the next, a fence post
Plays lookout tower to a bedraggled buzzard, eye turned in seeming toast
Acknowledging the red kite flying high overhead,
While on the road it has spotted roadkill; long dead.

Walking on, rain still gently falling, off waxen leaves beads and droplets roll.
Bisham church looms in the near distance, many years take their toll
On 12th century buildings standing still by Father Thames
I look across water where pads of lilies lolled in many river bends.

The season is now far gone and marginal plants are no longer at their best
Like grebes, no longer great, no longer sporting a proud bristling crest.
I'm left only with memories of banded demoiselles and damselflies
Now reality is muddy river paths, beneath burdened, leaden, heavy skies.

The COVID-19 pandemic rages on, perhaps lessening, and so social restrictions ease. I was ill, although it probably was not COVID, I did have some sort of post-viral syndrome for months. Exercise was difficult, I had chest pain and walking became my rehab. Getting walking again on pavements leading into countrified areas on the road leading out of Marlow. Looking for plants, insects, seeing farm fields and farm animals, red kites and buzzards, and even in late autumn, *Vespula vulgaris*, common wasps feeding on ivy nectar, and imagining other wildlife in the woodland in the distance and around the Thames beyond the line of houses on the road towards Bisham Church. It was sensory overload and I think the poem here reflects that, as it too is, arguably, 'too busy'!

Gaius Caligula

How wrong they of condemnative fever
To spurn and despise the divine Caesar.
When for pleasure enemies and friends he would torture
Enjoying their violent screams for mercy,
With a smile his thumb downward jerked.
The ecstasy therein to run down his spine
As with laughter he greeted every dying whine.

So, with his sisters raped, one beside him on his throne
A growing greater madness did he own.
And with this growth the foetus kicked inside her.
But no complete term of gestation served;
Caesar slit the conquered's belly
To gorge himself on the contents of the womb
Caligula's stomach to become its tomb.

As a Roman history 'buff', I enjoyed the BBC drama *I, Claudius*, with Derek Jacobi playing the lead role in the 1970s and later enjoyed the Robert Graves book too. It was memories of the TV series, and John Hurt's fantastically debauched and sociopathic portrayal of Caligula that inspired me to write about the infamous Roman Emperor. I had a copy of Suetonius' *The 12 Caesars* but honestly, I have not quite got around to reading it.

Pressure

Smother me with kisses,
Touch my lips with wine,
Fill my head with your desires,
But I cannot make them mine.

Relationships can be difficult and when wants and desires become mismatched between two people who are in a relationship, the road ahead can be rocky and or can end. This poem was me thinking about how I felt about the relationship I was in at the time. I had already decided I needed to end it and the writing of this poem allowed me to better order my thoughts. If poets honestly write poems about how they feel, they publicly wear their hearts on their sleeves and often this can reveal the state of the human mind, which is not always savoury or sanitary.

I am human and imperfect but it would be more dishonest, more cruel, to continue in a relationship where the other person has false hopes. In dealing face to face with the person when you are ending the relationship, you must be firm but with the kindness you would wish from others. I might think it, but I certainly would not express it to any person as I have in the poem.

Prowess Everlasting

Seek not the winds that burn my soul
For they will burn you also.
Peeling flesh for beasts to maul,
No place to hide; cave nor mountain tall.

So, face the foe as well you might
Let no demon-evil show you fright,
For you will spurn such weary pain
And stand your ground and fight.

Flesh torn from bone, yet still you fight
Blood coursing, you feel your body grow in might.
No dreadful fear can douse the flame,
To live forever is your aim.

There were times when I felt almost overwhelmed and this is one of a number of poems that were part of a strategy to identify the issues and turn my mood around.

Remission's End

Some may curse
And some may swear
And others; simply sit and stare
Yet when confronted by such news

One can only but react and muse
Is life fair or just, to end it all too soon?
Cancer shortens life and muddled minds confuse
Evil sprite make merry, but this can be no ruse.

Life of waste
With no attempt to savour taste.
Obsolete when famine bites
You are bitten and so bite.

My mother died of ovarian cancer at the very young age of 49, when I was 18. This poem is one that reflects my soul-searching and attempts to make sense of it. In addition, when you lose a parent, particularly when you and the parent are young, the futility of life looms large, you feel like you can only deal with the terror in front of you and so have no capacity to deal with issues higher up Maslow's hierarchy; namely, self-esteem and self-actualisation and in fact, you might 'lash-out'.

Four decades later, after having contact with thousands of people, I know my mother was a very good and caring person. Not perfect, no-one is, but she taught me so much about what is important in life, and all in a very short space of time. And of course, it has taken four decades for me to process it all, attempt to behave according to my mother's values and to recognise, value and be grateful for her and what she taught me.

The Hunted

Stark fear apparent
As he listens for the smallest of sounds.
Pupils dilated, cold sweat on his brow, heart beating in his throat.
The snap of a twig; adrenalin courses, prickling his skin.

Head cocked, straining to hear, or even feel, danger;
For danger it was …stalking him.
But although scared, he in perfect control; compassionless,
No life too valuable; sacrificed that he and his will survive.

Survival, his only aim,
For he must live, will live.
Nothing to lose, fear subsides,
Power replacing it, his scalp tingles in anticipation of the kill.

Another poem written and used to turn around my mood and fears.

Starbucks vs Costa

I sit in Starbucks,
Not my favourite coffee shop,
Jazz playing in the background,
Which would give my dad pleasure,
But it's 'corporate *Avant Garde*'
Perhaps to be enjoyed as a simple treasure?

I prefer Costa, on the adjacent street;
Encamped in a sixteenth century building
Yet often closed, due to plumbing, and staff, issues
But quieter with less distraction
And so there, I more easily read and write
Where I can compose in simple contemplation and reflection.

I do a lot of reading and writing in Costa in Marlow but due to its problems with staffing, plumbing and the Covid-19 pandemic, I was forced, for a few months, to use Starbucks instead. There, I am often irritated by higher noise levels, contributed to by children and even dogs. When I was a child, you were not allowed to take dogs into places where people were eating, they would be tied up outside. Not sure what changed and when it ceased to be thought a public health issue. But then perhaps, I am just grumpy, old and irritable!

Suicide?

To dance is a joy, with her.
To see the delight in her timeless eyes,
Her beautiful form and grace:
Taunting me.
Eyes sparkling, sweet breath,
Tenderness, love?
Will I ever know these, her qualities?

She, torn from my wretched mind,
Is but a breath of fresh air
Which fills my stale heart and brain.
May I never tire of her joyful being,
That I may someday show her the love
Within me that is rightly hers.

Destined; cursed forever to see,
Not to have.
Her tender lips,
If 'twere they touched mine
Would I in a frenzy of disbelief,
Gladly die, happy, content to save her from
Pain and sorrow.
So be it I die.

This is the very first poem I wrote, in my early teens, after being at the Christmas disco at my secondary school. I was smitten by this girl, convinced I was in love. I sent her a dozen red roses on her birthday which was in January(!) and I sat for hours on my own in front of our house phone placed on the kitchen table, trying to psyche myself up to phone her and ask her out on a date. When I finally got up the courage, she rejected me! This is where stand-up comedians get their material from and it was the start of an illustrious career in unrequited love! But in fairness, punctuated by some good luck too, although that came years later!

Decisions

I must find pastures anew,
For here stagnation is rampant.
Somewhere skies must be blue,
Where happiness flourishes
Where there isn't harassment.

Thoughts of escape: another poem suggesting poor mental health? Again, during my teenage years, the harassment mentioned was that of authority generally but especially from the authority of my parents. The constant feeling of having to do things you don't want to do, that you have to conform.

Land of Hope and Glory

Yet again I travel life's unending corridor,
With cauterised brain and anaesthetised emotions
And when I think of that which bothers me
I couldn't care less.

When to control conscious movement
Is too much trouble,
And so there I stand, a brainless vegetable
And content in that thought am I.

For many years after my mother died, I suspect I had depression, at times, clinical. I didn't know it at the time. I just felt there was something wrong with me. But at its worst, I didn't care about anything, least of all myself. There were times I would write poems through tears and I knew the more I was writing the more 'screwed-up' I was. But the need to get the feeling out, and at least partially, or for the time-being, put it aside, was ever present as if, to allow the thoughts to remain in my head, would damage or even, destroy me.

Armageddon Earth

The sun; a golden orb hung in the sky,
To mark the day mankind will die.
No-one cares to testify
To grace that day with reason.

Until that day we'll sit and sigh
With no-one here to wonder why.
A fated time will seal our doom
The dying Earth to become our tomb.

In the 1980s, the threat of atomic war seemed very real indeed. The Cold War between the East and the West represented largely by the superpowers on opposing sides, the USSR and the USA was largely political posturing. Both sides had huge stockpiles of nuclear weapons the rationale being that they acted as a deterrent to the opposite side starting anything. The news bulletins on TV referred to the enmeshed politics constantly and I guess contributed to the tension we all felt.

The worry was that some unhinged or arrogant leader might, in a despotic, megalomaniacal act start World War III, a nuclear war in which numerous retaliations would result in the wiping out the majority of life and the ultimate destruction of the planet. It affected popular culture too with films like 'War Games' and music, such as the song 'Two Tribes' by *Frankie Goes to Hollywood*.

The Truth of the Matter

I seek not martyrdom,
For in death I could not love her half as well
As in this shackled mortal hell
Where thoughts of her will always dwell
A-gnawing at all reason.

A poem of unrequited love, but which decries the notion of ending one's life in the name of love. I wrote here in what I saw as the style of a Shakespearian tragedy.

Winter...Discontent

Softly thoughts come to me
Some, like the approach of a cat on a carpet,
Others land like gentle summer rain drops
And trickle down the pain of my memory.

Memories one by one, drift back at first,
A downy feather floating across a puddle.
But soon fast in torrents wash
To mingle and become lost in my chattering mind.

Dark, damp, clean chestnut hair
Cool cascading across my chest
in contrast to the heat as our skin touches.
I sigh before forcing the images back;
I try not to revel long in pleasures lost

There lies madness when one lies alone.
An empty bed, so cold in winter
When long, dark nights
Mean fist-fighting melancholy.

A good relationship. I blew it! When I was young, perhaps I never knew what was good for me.

Årlanda

In bright sunlight
Aircraft stand at their gates
Quiet but for the activity
Of Day-Glo figures, fire-fly bright in the sun.

They load and unload, unheard through thick glass
And oblivious as a light breeze
Whips up powdery snow;
White horses race and break across a tarmac shore

Its black surface streaked cream and grey
With slush that refuses to melt further,
Where only a passing aircraft
Disturbs the view with heat haze from its engines.

After working in the Swedish Arctic with cross-country skiers, I got the train back to Stockholm, and then sat, fascinated at the departure gate at Årlanda airport, watching the preparation of my flight that would return me to London Heathrow. I never tired of watching a plane being sprayed nose to tail in anti-freeze! It was a novelty because it was something I had never witnessed in the maritime climate of the UK, and before travelling in Nordic countries, I never even knew it was a thing!

Death of a Loved One

The most beautiful girl in his world;
She died in his arms.
And with her last breath
The tears rolled down his face

The ache in his heart,
The disbelief in his mind
Left him numb,
Cold: insensitive to all around him.

He looked down on this beautiful form
Lying there still and quiet in his arms.
He held her close to his face.
His nose caught the perfumed fragrance of her hair.
Her cheek was still warm next to his.

Yet her chest no longer rose and fell
As it rapidly did when he made love to her.
He ran his index finger gently over her lips,
Then kissed her but she did not return his kiss.

And with her life
Was his flame for existence
Also extinguished.
Two lives and loves lost as one.

I wrote this after reading the book 'Dr Fischer of Geneva or The Bomb Party' by Graham Greene, which was also made into a film with James Mason, Alan Bates and Greta Scacchi. There was a scene in which the Alan Bates character witnesses the death of his wife following a skiing accident. I imagined what it must feel like to lose someone you love that way.

Masquerade

Calm the waters of your eyes
Though you boil within.
Make them think it's tears of joy you shed,
No satisfaction found in giving in.

Another poem which perhaps illustrates the state of a mind fighting depression. Nowadays, it is more acceptable for men to be seen shedding a tear or two. When I wrote this, it was still seen as a weakness and something to be ashamed of. Being unhappy or sad were not excuses.

High-Powered Dying

In the business world,
Fortunes lost and found.
Where midday meals clinch business deals
Mere mortals to confound.

Dog eat dog 'midst panic and confusion
On the stock-exchange companies labour and die.
Two survive with their fusion.
Out-of-work grown men cry.

A poem which examines the paradox of people in high-powered city jobs, the unspoken lack of an appropriate work-life balance.

New Guitar

An ambition realised
Held since I was a child
I hold my new guitar in my arms
And caress its voluptuous form.

Bought in Granada
Birthplace of the guitar.
With nylon strings and broad, hard wood neck
Rich in many ways.

Rich in smell; full, dark, peppery.
Rich in colour; lacquered, polished, orange wood.
Rich in feel; smooth, solidly made and good to hold.
Rich in tone; resonant and sweet.

A joy to my ear, eye, hand, nose and heart
A reason to go on
Such sweet sound and smell
Plays my soul alone.

At 19, I bought a cheap Spanish-style guitar (for £20, which was cheap even then!) from a music shop on Sauchiehall Street in Glasgow. I spent hours every day practicing and playing songs of the day, which I'd bought sheet music for (I could only ever 'read' the chord windows!). David Bowie and Beatles songs were great favourites and, honestly, I quickly reached the limits of my ability, beyond which I couldn't progress! However, I was good enough, at one point, that my best friend at the time, Paul, brought a girl round to my flat and got me to play and sing and use that to successfully 'woo' her.

One Easter, years later, I realised the ambition to buy a classical Spanish guitar in Granada. But, ironically (since the Granada-bought guitar was around ten times the value) I always preferred playing my original, cheap guitar. Frustration in not getting any better, meant I have not played for more than 20 years. But my guitar-playing too, was a refuge in difficult times and so is something I have fond memories of and I still enjoy guitar solos and in particular Spanish guitar music or phrases played in songs.

Frozen Winter Landscape

Trees laden with snow and frost
Heavy cold freezing fog lying in the hollows
Like thick white soup
But no satisfaction of thirst or hunger found there.

Only deep snow and deeper unrelenting cold
To chill the bones and freeze the marrow
Air laden with ice crystals, sparkling in the sunlight
Yet no warmth here, where you can feel your nose hair freeze.

And in a strange way I really like it.
Fascination smothering my normal dislike of cold.
But this deep, dry, desiccating cold
Differs greatly from the damp, damp cold of home.

In my travels, working with elite athletes, I was always fascinated by cold, snow and frosty landscapes.

Business Tide

Fog and misty morning.
Oppressed slow rising sun
Casting warm half-light
Across a damp dormant winter kissed land.

Trees their silhouette-black trunks and brown leaves
Muslin shrouded, barely seen.
Poplars now; leave less, diffuse forms
Fingers pointing skyward.

A green and brown patchwork of fields
Stretching far, pale-etched with frost.
Rural grey stone churches
Steal a mediaeval glance across the land.

Steam rising from the slow
Meander of a river.
Crow on the wing, straight-line flying
Making for a group of trees on the near horizon.

And the train,
Hurtling on ram-rod tracks.
Walking passengers lurch, thrown from side to side.
Men working on their laptops
Ebb and flow of business tide.

On an early morning train journey, I was struck by the number of businessmen who seemed to be commuters and who, clearly made this long journey every day. It seemed something of a drudge to me, a life like that, but perhaps, for many the way they made a living. But often with heads buried in a newspaper, they missed the beautiful, rapidly changing scenes of nature passing by which had me transfixed.

North Star

Walk with me in sunshine,
Walk with me in rain.
Hold me, feel my heart beat
Tell me your love will always be the same.

For you I'll climb the mountain,
But you hold up the skies.
For you I'll swim the torrent,
Whilst you calm all the seas.

I hold your hand in mine,
In yours you hold my heart.
You are my true north star
And from your love, I never wish to part.

A poem of out-and-out love that is constructed from feelings from a number of past relationships and/or in the early 'honeymoon' period in every new relationship. For many, this love exists in the here-and-now. I am envious and happy for them.

Max

I miss you my brother
Your sleek black fur
Calmed me as I stroked you
And listened to you purr.

When I talked and called to you
Your face in seeming smile
You blinked with warm affection
Before sauntering in my direction

And I crouched down
So you might butt my head
Smell my nose
And rub cheek and flank against my shoulder.

As a kitten your paw chased
The sheepdog in 'One Man and His Dog'
As you sat atop the TV
Eyes brightly sparkling, tail twitching.

You often came chirruping
When our Mother called
As her stroke to you
Was your greatest reward.

And when she died
I know you felt and respected our grief
Sensitive to all of us who loved and raised you
That bond with you I still feel now.

Max is the cat we got as a kitten, perhaps two years before my mum died. He was her cat and would call to her with a chirruping sound and come running when she called in response. My mum was baking in the kitchen one day and she dropped a small plastic pastry cutter, which rolled across the floor. Max ran after it and brought it back in his mouth to her feet.

After that, we used a small cotton reel and threw it for Max to play with and bring back. When my mum died, Max transferred his affection to my dad. Dad was a dentist in a poorer part of Glasgow where, once a week, a van would drive through the neighbourhood selling fish. My dad would interrupt this work to rush out, buy fish and cook it in the surgery kitchen to take home for Max at lunchtime. After lunch, Dad would have '40 winks' and Max would sit on his chest—Max eyes closed and purring and Dad asleep and snoring.

The 'New' Royal Opera House, Covent Garden

The portals and cloistered alleys
Of Covent Garden are abuzz
With heady excitement,
A throbbing, palpable as a heartbeat.

The new ROH proud in one corner
Seems to lead the soul-felt vibrations
As a great conductor leads the orchestra
This symphony, just begun, is rising to crescendo.

To enter this great architectural wonder
Mouth agape, eyes drinking such beauty
And once inside an atmosphere of thrill
Heavy as humid honeysuckle breeze, sticky and fresh as dew.

The Opera House in Covent Garden was completely refurbished and the result was architecturally stunning and there was a real buzz in the streets the day they reopened it. I was lucky enough to be in Covent Garden that day.

Smell

My mother's sense of smell was that of legend.
When she enquired of us all 'do you smell something burning?'
We knew not to question but to search high and low
And inevitably found her sense founded in discovery.

My own sense of smell is but a fraction
Of that legendary whole
And yet I have often relied on it
And know it to be better than that of others.

I often notice the smell of damp in the air
Before the rain comes
Or know of so and so's passing
For the lingering of an odour uniquely theirs.

Even cologne is made unique
By its intermingling with the individual's own body chemistry
And such an identifier is as singular as
A fingerprint, palm print, retinal scan or sample of DNA.

The memories which smell evoke
Are so vivid and unique to that sense.
None of the other special senses stir
Memory nor imagination so strongly.

When I smell honeysuckle or jasmine
I see beautiful Mediterranean islands
And feel the sun's warmth on my bare skin,
My mood brightens and blooms.

Yet only honeysuckle reminds me of childhood
Of summer in our garden
Where, by the front steps,
Bees were attracted by the heavy, warm scent.

Only smell can evoke memories
Of times long since forgotten
And recreate the scene
In every aspect and hue,

Conjuring even the breeze and temperature
The colour of the day; painted in sky and mood.
Enhancing daily life
And making palatable all food.

It's true, my mother had an amazing sense of smell! Research has demonstrated that of all our special senses, smell is probably the most linked to memory and that is why a smell can aid in recalling a memory.

Writing

With pen in hand I realise
Writing is not always easy.
Sporadic, impulsive, rarely planned
Good writing plumbs the depths of feeling.

And like the ocean, one must retreat
To the deepest, darkest void
To find that which is most highly prized
But even then, nothing is certain.

Even pain, discomfort, fear
Is no guarantee.
But I have always written best
At my lowest ebb.

When fear, pain, frustration erode my life
And suicide beckons I feel in technicolour
And can relate feelings
With so much greater clarity.

But must I really plumb such depths
To find inspiration that others
Can relate to?
I have other plans.

I've been interested in writing and the written word for years. Working in academia, we have to publish research as part of our contract of employment. In physiology, this generally is done in around 4,000 words. This leaves little room to be creative in the use of language and so can, in my view, result in writing which is quite sterile, dry, stilted even. It wasn't always like this. The British Nobel Laureate, AV Hill, who jointly won the prize for Physiology or Medicine in 1922, wrote very entertainingly indeed.

So, to me it became apparent that you can write, conforming to the strict concise requirements of published scientific research but I also wanted to try to cultivate and own other styles of writing too. As a result, I try to be more creative and to enjoy the written word and written expression in many styles, including song lyrics. For example, check out 'Make You Feel My Love' by Bob Dylan. Adele released a beautiful cover version.

Other examples from further back: 'Crazy' by Willie Nelson, made famous by Patsy Cline or 'I will always love you', written by Dolly Parton but it was Witney Houston's version, from the soundtrack of the film 'The Bodyguard,' that sold millions and brought it to several new audiences. There are numerous other examples; lyrics of Bernie Taupin set to music and sung by Elton John over many decades. The list is endless and I haven't even mentioned any of the poetry classics yet!

Childhood Rain

As a child I'd sit,
Back against the tumble dryer,
Watching the clothes in the washing machine
In a dream. Warm.

Gazing occasionally through
The window to see rain,
And constant transient circles in growing puddles
Day on endless day.

My overwhelming memory of a childhood in Glasgow was perpetual grey and incessant rain. The poem above is a memory of sitting in the house unable to go out because it rained non-stop for four days straight.

Christmas Flight

The cabin crew serve breakfast
And my stomach is finally appeased.
I wish I could say the same for my ears
Assaulted for the duration
By the woman with the megaphone voice,
Seated by the window.

I try to feel sympathetic
Perhaps she has a hearing disorder.
Surreptitious glances looking for a hearing aid
Are fruitless …She is just noisy.
Sympathies evaporate,
She continues to irritate.

For years, I have worked in the SE of England and perhaps went home to Glasgow two or three times a year, the most notable of which was Christmas. Clearly, I am irritable and grumpy here!

Addict

Starving for affection
Waiting to be fed
Together we can banquet
In my lonely bed.

Perhaps risqué. Clearly, I had been without female company for a while!

Doctorate

Wonder, awe …excitement.
Frustration, pain, distraction.
Almost a decade of stop-start journeys
None yet ended with a PhD.

Science still captivates;
The more I learn, the more I realise
How little I know and,
The more I want to know.

But hard-earned nuggets
Of knowledge must be won little by little
With diligence, patience and fighting off frustration
Was it ever thus, my education.

After my mum died, I took a while to grow up and I failed two undergraduate degree courses. I had to work as a swimming coach and lifeguard for 3 years before finally getting into the University of Glasgow and successfully completing a BSc in Physiology and Sports Science.

Years later, I registered for 3 PhDs but all were curtailed as a result of Olympic politics and I finally started PhD study proper in 2000 and successfully completed it and was awarded the qualification in 2003. I was always interested in science, natural history, sport and exercise and I have been able to combine two of these as a career and keep the other as a hobby.

After many years dominated by failure, obtaining a degree and then a PhD would have surprised my mum. Despite my many failures and negative reviews at many school parents' evenings, she still believed I would achieve and be successful in life. It makes me happy to believe she would be surprised and thrilled that I have exceeded the views of many people.

Holocaust Memorial

Repeated sharp cracks
Echo from a clearing
In a Balkan forest
As the last flake of snow falls
With the last dying breath.

Once kneeling figures
Now lie sprawled in the trench below.
Unseeing eyes staring skyward
A single hole in the back of the head.

A spray of blood amongst many on once white snow
Now pink stained.
On the sides and bottom of the trench darker red
Blood oozing from the wounds of the newly dead.

The SS doing their duty.
Uniforms and hands stained with blood
Clear conscience, following orders,
Protecting the Aryan race.

But how is such horror
Justified in the minds of men?
To allow evil to be enacted
And to reduce people to that of sub-human.
More than half a century later
The old remember
And cry at the memory
As scars are re-opened.

But thankfully only temporarily
As victims are remembered
So that the World will never forget
Lest such crimes are again perpetrated.

Every year, Holocaust Memorial Day marks a terrible time in history and the stories of the six million murdered Jews continue to horrify. In some quarters of the world, fascist views rise again and, with it, Holocaust denial but also lurking is the danger that we might forget, risking similar atrocities in the future. That made me want to write this.

Ignorance Across Millenia

The Ottoman army blowing the nose off the Sphinx.
The Venetian fleet landing a mortar on the Parthenon.
French archers using Da Vinci's model horse for target practice.
Acts of bad taste, barbarism, ignorance all.

How many other acts of wanton destruction,
Carried out over millennia,
Now deprive present and future peoples
Of the beauty and awe of the treasures of antiquity?

The rhetorical answer saddens and angers.
Such acts devalue humanity
Reducing to vandalism
A state of mind-numbness, the last word in dumbing down.

Desecration of ancient culture continues today and needs to stop. The religious views of others shouldn't be used to justify the destruction of culture or of sites that should be seen as belonging to the whole of humanity.

Letters

Those letters which lie
In isolated patches in various parts of my house,
Scare me.
They were read once and lie there still,
Left untouched ever since.

I fear picking them up, or even touching them.
I know I would be compelled to read.
A reminder of the compassion, love
And understanding she held me in.

A reminder too of the lack of real value
I attached to one so warm and caring.
I do not wish to feel the pain that dwells in that carelessness
And so, they remain untouched.

Content forgotten. Yet they do call.
Curiosity touches me.
But I am aware they are a Pandora's Box
Opened and pain and hurt will be unleashed.

I do not know why I behaved so
But I do regret it
And resolve to reciprocate appropriately
Should I ever be loved again.

If you live a full life, it is perhaps impossible not to have a few regrets. No one is perfect and so it is easy to make mistakes, to be selfish, to hurt others. And so perhaps, having a few regrets should be the normal state for normal people who live full lives! But this should not stop us trying to do the right thing; to be kind, to be compassionate, to try to resist the selfish default that characterises most of us.

Biathlon: The Build-Up Begins

Short sharp breathing
Interrupted briefly for the repeated cracks of a rifle.
The smell of cordite hangs heavy here by the range
Before the athlete once again skis off for another circuit.

Smooth glide on the flat
Uphill the stride changes
And the 'lub dub' gait echoes heart rhythm
But in that movement the heart sound is faster, more urgent.

Never ending incline causes chest and muscle burn.
Years of training, season upon season has tempered the body
With endurance few can match
A passion for success, that elusive gold to catch.

For a few years, I worked closely with British biathletes (cross-country skiing and shooting) in the lead-up to the Winter Olympics. I travelled with the team and attended the Olympics as an accredited assistant coach and sports scientist. Biathlon is a 'Nordic' event and is impressive on many counts, but not least because, often, the shooting range is reached after skiing up an incline. Athletes take up their positions and must consciously bring their heart rate down from its 180bpm peak and shoot between heartbeats to avoid the vibration of the end of the muzzle caused by the pressure wave of blood that comes with each heartbeat. It remains unclear how athletes are able to shoot between beats!

Wreck

Anchor chain encrusted with rich red rust
Bright, warm… attractive in the sunlight
Of an isolated beach cove
A cargo vessel out of commission for more than 50 years

Its red hull stained in a few places
With the hint of gun-metal blue,
A coastal steamer, its funnel askew
No longer smoking, now silent, now dead

Like the fossilised bones
Of some long extinct organism
Barely recognisable
Only a leap of faith, conjured imagination bringing it to
ghostly life.

I saw a picture of a rusty wreck on a beautiful beach somewhere and, for some reason I was "transported" there and wrote this poem about it.

Travel at Night

A bus winds, glow-worm slow,
Along darkening country roads
Towards a destination
That I will never know.

But humans unique, ubiquitous
Are everywhere
And travel to each niche
Is transport familiar in nationwide pastiche.

Yet another occasion when I was travelling on a train; this time to visit family in Scotland. I have mainly flown to Scotland on my frequent visits because train travel is slow and expensive. The upside is the fact you get to see scenery and a glimpse of life across the country. On this occasion, I saw this scene in darkening twilight.

Phoenix

In that cold winter madness
A wind blew in from Hell.
To suck the breath and steal the soul
To vent on us a terrible toll.

Yet from the wrath
Resolve was born
A strength that grew
Banishing looks forlorn.

So, turn the tide
Live life with pride
Be bold and sure, humble and pure
Advance in confident measured stride
That ever will your will abide.

Another poem aimed at turning mood around when the biathlon team I was part of did not receive the support it deserved and so we all had to rely on each other as the Olympic approached. Bear in mind elite athletes make sacrifices, including spending less time with friends and family, over many years and so it is important, particularly for mental health and long-term happiness that the sacrifice has been 'worth it'!

Silk

A quiet, sombre man sits, dark eyes fixed on mine.
A beautiful young woman lies with her head in his lap
He, stroking her dark shiny hair. She, with eyes closed.
The stark minimalist room a study in monochrome.

Save for the shiny silk scarlet dress she wears
Covering her whole body: blanket-like
Where she lies on the floor.
Unmoving, unreal.

My eyes fall on hers
And in that instant her eyes open revealing
Piercing bright blue chips of sapphire
Holding my awestruck gaze.

Touch my heart.
Capture my soul.
Ignite my wildest spirit.
Life and love could never be the same again.
To yearn and burn until I know not when.

I read a very interesting fictional book of the same title, all about trading in silk worms and Europeans encountering new cultures and politics in nineteenth century Japan. The main protagonist ended up having a relationship with the Japanese nobleman's concubine. That section of the book stimulated this poem.

GB Biathlon

Stout men are they
To plunge headlong into the fray
When some would scorn
Still to battle are they sworn.

To stand despite the odds
Lungs ache with exertion and cold
Hereafter, in hearth-front,
Their bold exploits will be told.

Men of honour, men of steel
No thoughts of quitting do they feel
To challenge so they rise
In search of that elusive prize.

Competing in elite Nordic skiing events is a very tough business, requiring the height of aerobic conditioning, following years of training 4-5 hours per day. GB athletes are few and far between and almost always come from the armed forces and first get the chance to try cross-country skiing at the age of sixteen or seventeen. It is a highly technical sport too and it takes many years to become competent. The Scandinavians in particular are very proficient technically and their elite skiers are very fit. They have more than a decade head-start on the Brits as they start skiing very young, and we do not.

Fully Laden Travel

A faint shadow of blue
Cast on skin over rib
A testament to blows and bangs
Of luggage held too close.

To travel thus
Full burden on each limb
A once brawny back
That now yearns not to give in.

I often travelled on my own as the GB athletes would have been training at my destination for weeks and I would be going to either support competition or to check up how things were going, that therefore monitoring training. That therefore meant travelling with quite a lot of equipment—heavy and difficult to manage.

Canada Beckons

On and on towards
A barely breaking dawn
Westward, ever westward ho
Throw caution to the wind
In light and shadow we go.

A cold clear land from windows we spy
Ice and snow on mountain,
Winds across the plains cry.
A mournful sound, a dirge for a Summer long gone
Sun weak and faint casts light upon wildlife forlorn.

Long haul travel again but not on my own; this time to Canada with the GB Biathlon squad where we would train for two weeks before flying south to Salt Lake City for the Winter Olympics. We stayed in log cabins in Engadine National Park. At night you could see wolves and elk on the other side of the valley in moonlight almost as bright as day. At the start of each day I'd go for a run down the Smith Dorrien Highway; a four-lane, dirt-track highway.

On one morning, 200m ahead on a poker-straight part of the road, I watched a moose wander onto the road and stop and stare in my direction. It then wandered across the width of the road and into the trees. By the time I reached the spot, there was no sign that a 10-foot-tall animal had been there.

The Wait

Mile after trudging mile, walking over
Mizzle-shrouded rolling hills,
Steepening into the mountains
Passing tarns, negotiating bogs

Fighting fatiguing limbs and aching joints
Aware of every heart-pounding iamb.
At destination, camping each night
And waiting quietly all day just observing, waiting.

And now the rain has come
Cold from the north-east, even now in summer,
Pounding the peat bog which hisses quietly as it soaks up the rain
And then quiet, broken only by the sheep's bleat

Or the far-off soaring screech of the golden eagle,
The wheeling, throaty, rasping caw of the raven.
The weather alternates between rain and mizzle
And still all day just observing, waiting.

Four days, six days, ten and then
Through clearing mist; the prize
A rare bird to these shores spotted and recorded
After days of all-day observing, watching; waiting.
Such is the life of the field naturalist,
Or of the wildlife photographer,
To endure in silent isolation
Days of all-day observing, watching; waiting.

We are very lucky to see such fantastic wildlife documentaries in our time. David Attenborough programmes are amongst the best. Some scientists feel his approach is to personify and endow animals and plants with the same feelings and thoughts that humans have and that this is wrong because as species we are bound to differ, often enormously. But how can we be sure what animals feel or think? Frans De Waal, Professor of Psychology at Emory University in Atlanta, Georgia suggests in this book 'Are we smart enough to know how smart animals are?' that those who anthropomorphise may not be entirely wrong to do so. Whether valid criticism or not, none can deny the education and awareness Attenborough has brought to millions.

The technology and dedication of naturalists, scientists, of cameramen and camera women. These people often endure great hardship to find out about wildlife, to understand their place in the living world and to communicate it to the rest of us. We are now occasionally seeing glimpses of the difficulties these people encounter as many wildlife documentaries have a 10-15 minutes piece, at the end of each programme, amounting to a diary of those who made it.

Arctic Call

I hear the icecap calling
In every fibre bawling,
A far-off, whale-song sound
Echoing through the valleys of my mind.

I dream of cold white mountains
And of valleys with pristine, virgin snow
Cold-stretching far beyond the sight of man
The cares of civilisation no longer on show.

A map, flight traced over Greenland
Stimulates the imagination of that trip
Of grit and verve, of pain approached gung-ho
But no easy venture, not one for mere show.

Snow and ice were features that occupied my working environment and my dreams for a considerable period.

Flag

Wind whipping spray
From a rain drenched flag
While stark against the grey
A cold, wet, dank winter day.

A windy, rainy day in England, I noticed the Olympic flag outside the British Olympic Medical Centre.

At Byron's Grave

Atop a winding hill
Where Byron lay and lies there still
Beneath the drooping elm now bare
Where he lay in life, and thought without a care.

That place is peaceful still
Myriad birdsong, all around the hill.
Breeze rustles still, through brown dead leaves
Weak warm sunshine here in winter can deceive.

And to his Scottish birth be true
In contrast, from this hill a landscape flat he did view.
His heart and mine here can soar
Way above the traffic's roar.

Professor Craig Sharp was a founder of the British Olympic Medical Centre. Craig, who is sadly no longer with us, was originally a vet and was shortlisted for a Nobel Prize as a result of his PhD work. He was also a very good athlete; he was a semi-professional squash player in his younger days and he set the record for the fastest ascent of Kilimanjaro. He had also taught pathology and physiologist as an academic staff member at the University of Glasgow's vet school.

He switched interests from veterinary medicine to sports science, being the first ever lecturer in the subject in the 1970s, at Birmingham University and he was frankly, a polymath (an expert in many different things), he had an interest in poetry and had once been paid professionally as a poetry critic. We also share the fact that we are Scots and we were both working at the BOMC which was in Harrow and at Harrow on the Hill, in Harrow School's churchyard, is Byron's grave. Craig took me there to see it and that we might reminisce about Scotland, the place of our and Byron's birth.

The Truth Will Out

We stood together
Warriors on the edge of change.
And for two months lived with the thrill
Of believing we could change the world.
But corruption beat us back.
The battle lost, defeat the bitterest pill.
Yet in my heart the truth lives on,
And we will rise to confront them with that truth.
In years to come when their defence
Is seen for what is; weak and insubstantial.
They will quake and they will wail
But we rise above their faces pale
When they turn their backs on the World in attempted shun
For us, reunited, a long-lost battle will be won.

Since we, as Team GB, often competed against nations with a long history of Nordic skiing, which we didn't share, realistically we were always aiming to have our Olympic Nordic skiers finish in the top half of the field. Our Nordic skiers tend to be those who learn to ski as soldiers, and so only from the age of sixteen or seventeen. Britain too, however, has a very big stake in Olympic Games—the founder of the modern Olympics, Baron Pierre De Coubertin, derived the ethos for them from the English public-school system, and military pride is at stake too and comes with a specific culture. These two worlds together generate a lot of politics and the GB Olympic movement was still then, weirdly, locked in a 'Days of Empire' mentality. Navigating this politics was not easy and, frankly, our skiers were treated quite badly. In an attempt to help them, I came into conflict with 'the system' and a year after 'taking a stand', I was made redundant. At that point, I left the world of elite sport and entered that of academia.

Farewell

So now I say "Farewell!"
To leave no light on in this hell.
One day, here will lie bleaching bones
Cast off the dark, the sound of despairing moans.
Turn to a garden, warmed by sunlight,
A bright fresh day, heaped with marvel and delight
With morning dew upon the grass,
A better perspective will reign, the heavy mood will pass.
I will look back without burden, without care
And smell the perfume on another's hair.
I will look to my home in the Northwest
When battle is won, when I end my quest.
And there to stand in hope and love,
Meeting all the World with the whitest dove.

Putting years of unhappiness and, arguably, mental health issues behind me. 'Bleaching bones' refers to leaving pain far in the past. 'Leave no light on in this hell…' refers to not 'feeding' present problems. Lines 6/7 is about turning and dwelling on the positives in life and taking pleasure in that life. Lines 8/9/10 are about leaving the issues of my childhood and early adulthood in the West of Scotland behind and having no residual negative feelings when I return there in the future. The remaining four lines are about leaving past 'woes' behind, the possibility of finding love and of living in peace.